SEP − 5 2012

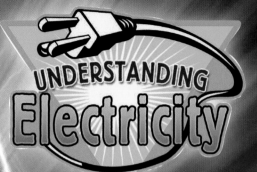

What Are
Electrical Circuits?

Ronald Monroe

Crabtree Publishing Company

www.crabtreebooks.com

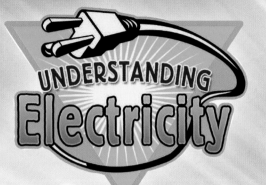

IMPORTANT
All experiments in this book can
be conducted by children. When
working with electricity, however, it
is always recommended that children
work with adult supervision.

Author: Ronald Monroe
Publishing plan research and development:
 Sean Charlebois, Reagan Miller
 Crabtree Publishing Company
Project development: Clarity Content Services
Project management: Karen Iversen
Editor: Rachel Eagen
Copy editor: Francine Geraci
Proofreader: Kathy Middleton
Photo research: Linda Tanaka
Design: First Image
Cover design: Margaret Amy Salter, Ken Wright
Production coordinator: Ken Wright
Prepress technician: Ken Wright
Print coordinator: Katherine Berti

Illustrations:
Chandra Ganegoda

Photographs:
cover Thinkstock, shutterstock; p1 JNT Visual/shutterstock;
p4 Philip Lange/shutterstock; p5 top marekuliasz/
shutterstock, Rodolfo Arpia/ shutterstock; p10 top
iStockphoto/ Thinkstock, HamsterMan/shutterstock; p11
David Asch/shutterstock; p12 VikramRaghuvanshi/
iStockphoto; p14 Digital Vision/ Thinkstock; p15 top
Russell Shively/ shutterstock, Steve Snowden/
shutterstock; p17 Amos Morgan/Thinkstock; p18
iceninephoto/iStockphoto; p19 top Shmeliova Natalia/
shutterstock, nullplus/iStockphoto; p20 top iStockphoto/
Thinkstock, NASA/Goddard Space Flight Center Scientific
Visualization Studio; p21 top Denton Rumsey/shutterstock,
Daniel Schwen/CCL/ Wikipedia; p22 Lisa F. Young/
shutterstock; p23 Jason Lugo/iStockphoto; p24 Arogant/
shutterstock; p26 Stellajune3700/iStockphoto; p27 Freddy
Eliasson/ shutterstock; p28 top Georgi Roshkov/
shutterstock, noolwlee/shutterstock; p29 cybrain/
shutterstock.

Library and Archives Canada Cataloguing in Publication

Monroe, Ronald D.
 What are electrical circuits? / Ronald Monroe.

(Understanding electricity)
Includes index.
Issued also in electronic format.
ISBN 978-0-7787-2077-5 (bound).--ISBN 978-0-7787-2082-9 (pbk.)

 1. Electric circuits--Juvenile literature. I. Title.
II. Series: Understanding electricity (St. Catharines, Ont.)

TK148.M56 2012   j621.319'2   C2012-901502-4

Library of Congress Cataloging-in-Publication Data

CIP available at Library of Congress

Crabtree Publishing Company
www.crabtreebooks.com   1-800-387-7650

Printed in Canada/042012/KR20120316

Published in Canada
Crabtree Publishing
616 Welland Ave.
St. Catharines, ON
L2M 5V6

Published in the United States
Crabtree Publishing
PMB 59051
350 Fifth Avenue, 59th Floor
New York, New York 10118

Published in the United Kingdom
Crabtree Publishing
Maritime House
Basin Road North, Hove
BN41 1WR

Published in Australia
Crabtree Publishing
3 Charles Street
Coburg North
VIC 3058

Contents

What Are Electrical Circuits?

Have you ever enjoyed an afternoon racing model cars? It is exciting to watch the cars race around and around the track. Did you know that a racetrack is a circuit?

Electrical Circuits

A circuit is a route that starts and finishes at the same place. An electrical circuit provides a pathway for **electrons** to flow. They flow from a power source, such as a battery, and through a **conductor**, such as copper wire. The circuit must be closed, with no breaks, for the electrons to flow.

Alternating and Direct Current

Some circuits carry **alternating current**. In alternating current, electrons vibrate back and forth in the circuit wires. Our buildings have wire circuits that deliver electricity to lights and outlets. Many of our household electrical items are powered by alternating current.

A stove's element, or burner, is a thick metal circuit that heats up when alternating current passes through it.

Other circuits carry **direct current**. In direct current, electrons move through the circuit in one direction. Many of our personal electronics, such as cell phones and tablet computers, use direct current.

The circuits in MP3 players are powered by direct current from batteries.

How Do You Make a Circuit?

When you turn on a light switch, you are completing an electrical circuit. This lets electrons flow from the power source to the bulb.

Try It for Yourself!

Experiment

Build a simple electrical circuit to make a bulb light up.

Materials

- 2 12-inch (20 cm) lengths of coated wire, 1 inch (2 cm) of each end exposed
- 1 battery
- 1 small light bulb

Procedure

1. Try connecting the wires, battery, and light bulb in different ways.
2. Connect one wire from the negative end of the battery to the light. Connect another wire from the light to the positive end of the battery.

Always work with an adult when you are experimenting with electricity.

What Happened and Why

Did you find a way to light the bulb? Look at the diagram. The wires connect the poles, or ends, of the battery to the light bulb. This completes the circuit and lights the bulb!

The wires connected to the battery are conductors. They make a circuit, letting the electrons flow from the negative pole of the battery, through the bulb, and finally to the positive pole of the battery.

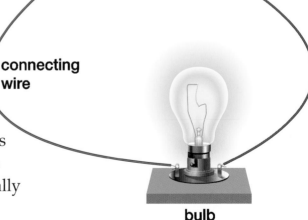

battery

connecting wire

bulb

Can Any Material Make a Circuit?

Metal wire works well in electrical circuits. Will other substances work?

Try It for Yourself!

Experiment

Try to make an electrical circuit using other materials.

Materials

⚡ 2 12-inch (20 cm) lengths of string
⚡ 1 battery
⚡ 1 small light bulb

Procedure

1. Make the circuit from the previous experiment, this time using string instead of wire.
2. Try making the circuit from other items, such as plastic straws or wooden chopsticks.

What Happened and Why

No matter how you connect the string, wood, or plastic, the bulb will not light. Electrons do not flow well through these materials. Substances that will not let electrons flow through them are called **insulators**. Insulators are wrapped around conductors to keep electrons from traveling where they are not wanted.

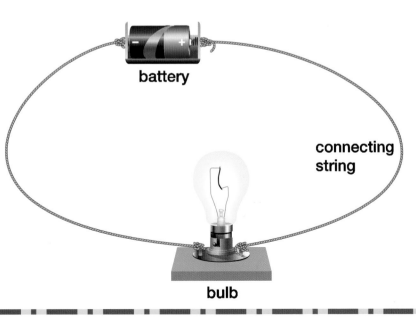

battery

connecting string

bulb

What Are the Parts of a Circuit?

Every electrical circuit has four parts, which are used to create simple or complex circuits.

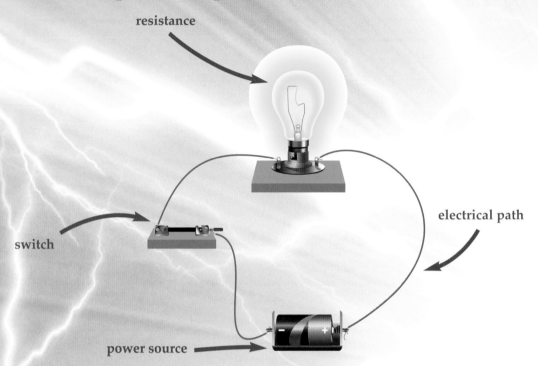

resistance

switch

electrical path

power source

The diagram shows the four parts of a simple circuit. Most electronic devices and electrical appliances have more than one circuit in them.

Power source: In this circuit, the battery pushes electrons through the wire. **Generators** provide electrons for the power lines that bring electricity to our homes.

Resistance: A **resistance** is a light, heating element, motor, or other electrical device that changes electrons into a different form of energy. To be useful, electricity needs to be changed into light, heat, or mechanical (motion) energy. Sometimes the resistance is called the **load**.

Electrical path: An electrical path is the route electrons travel in a circuit. Copper wire is a common material used for electrical paths because it is a good conductor.

Switch: A **switch** is a break in a circuit. When you flip or turn the switch, you either open or close the circuit. In many machines, switches turn on and off automatically.

Schematic Diagrams

Engineers and electricians who design electrical items and string electrical wire in houses use **schematic** diagrams. Schematic diagrams use symbols to represent circuit parts. This makes the plans easy to read.

Look at this schematic of the circuit on page 8. The lines represent the wires. What symbols represent the battery, resistance, and switch?

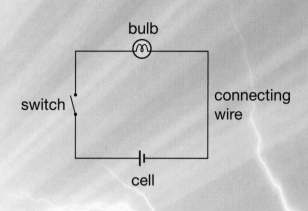

Common Schematic Symbols

Battery	⊣ǀǀǀǀ⊢
Bulb	
Cell	⊣ǀ⊢
Circuit breaker	S_{CB}
Outlet	
Resistor	
Switch, closed	
Switch, open	
Wire crossing, not joined	
Wires joined	

The table shows some of the common symbols used in schematic diagrams of circuits.

Many more symbols are used to represent complicated electronic circuits.

Flash fact

A cell is the simplest form of battery. Most batteries are made of a number of cells. Cells are easy to see in a car battery.

What Are Open, Closed, and Short Circuits?

Electricity must be controlled to be safe and useful. We keep it safely contained in wires by coating the wires with insulation. We also use switches to control the movement of electricity.

Open and Closed Circuits

An open circuit is an incomplete electrical path. A closed circuit is a complete path. Switches open and close circuits.

Electrons are always ready to travel. When you turn on a light switch, you close the circuit, allowing electrons to flow from the wires behind the wall, through the wires in the electrical path, and into the light source.

Complex electronics usually have many electrical circuits. Switches in these complicated circuits turn on and off automatically. They carry out their tasks on their own to make the device work.

An LED TV has a set of complex circuits positioned behind its screen. LED, which stands for "light-emitting diode," is a light source.

Flash fact

So they will start up quickly, many electronics have circuits that always have small amounts of electricity flowing through them, even when turned off.

Short Circuits

Electricity wants to follow the easiest and shortest path. If electrical wires are close together and are missing some of their insulation, electrons might jump from one wire to the other. This creates a short circuit.

Short circuits are dangerous. If a short circuit happens in household wiring, it can create a spark that could cause a fire. Luckily, wiring in houses connects through a **breaker** box. If a short circuit circuit occurs, the breaker will open. This stops the spark and prevents a fire.

Electricity always tries to find the shortest route back to the ground. If something like a ladder or even a kite on a string makes contact between a power line and the ground, a dangerous short circuit can occur. This can seriously injure or kill the person holding the ladder or kite.

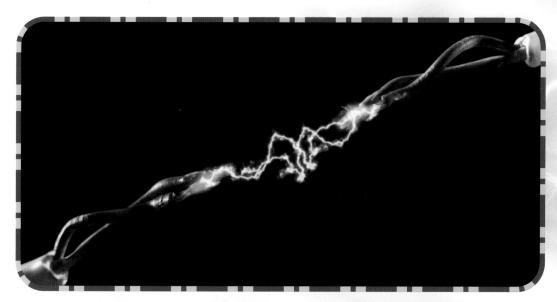

A short circuit spark between two wires can cause dangerous fires.

Lightning, which is a stream of electrons, also tries to find the shortest path to Earth. Lightning will often strike metal objects or objects wet from rain, because metal and water are better conductors than air.

Flash fact

What Is a Series Circuit?

A series circuit **has only one pathway for electrical current to flow. The electricity flows through one resistance, to the second resistance, to the third resistance, one after the other in a series.**

Try It for Yourself!

Experiment

How do you build a series circuit?

Materials

- battery
- copper wires
- switch
- 3 or 4 bulbs

Procedure

1. Begin by building a basic circuit like you did on page 6.
2. Fasten wires to the connectors on the switch. Turn on the switch.
3. Add a second bulb, connecting it as shown in the illustration shown below.
4. Turn on the switch and watch what happens.

Continue with the procedure on the next page.

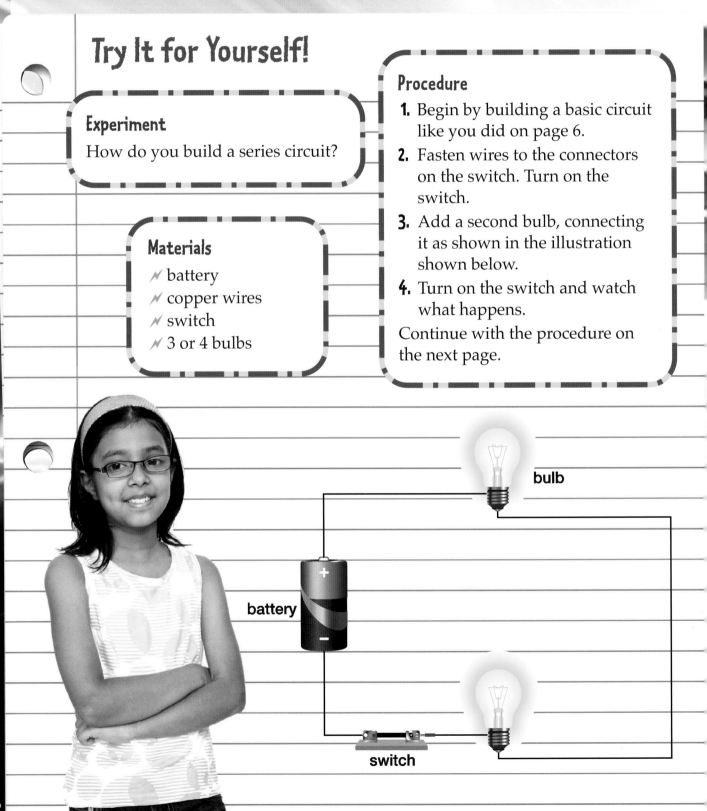

bulb

battery

switch

Procedure

5. Wire in a third bulb.

6. Turn the switch on and notice how much light the bulbs give off.

7. If you have a fourth bulb, you might even wire it in and observe.

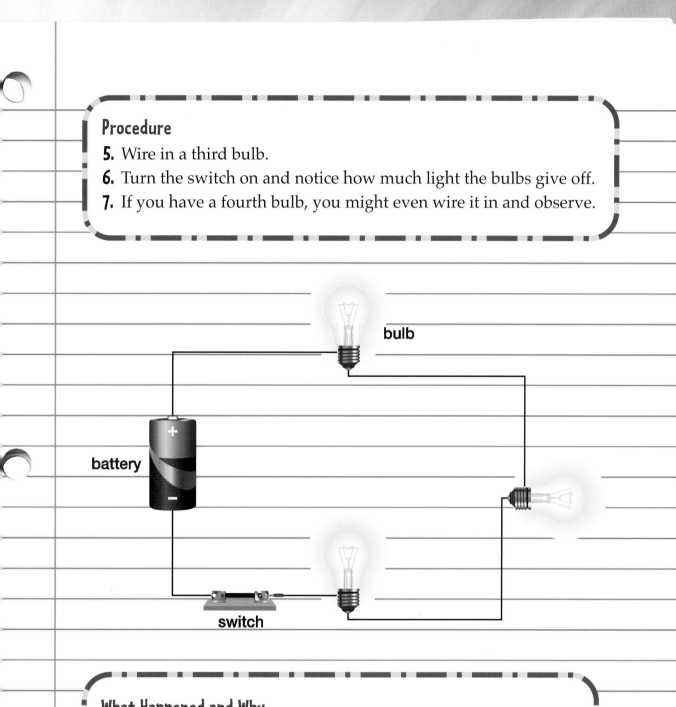

What Happened and Why

The bulbs appear one after the other along the circuit. When you added a second and a third bulb to the circuit, the bulbs shone less brightly. Bulbs in a series share the electricity that moves through the one wire.

How Do We Use Series Circuits?

Series circuits are used when it is important that everything in the circuit is on or off at the same time.

Lighting

A light switch is connected in series with the lights it controls. When the switch is off, all the lights on the circuit are off. When the switch is turned on, all the lights are on.

Some tree lights are wired as a series circuit. If one bulb burns out, the circuit is opened and all the lights go out.

This schematic shows a series circuit. Can you identify the breaker box, a switch, and two lights?

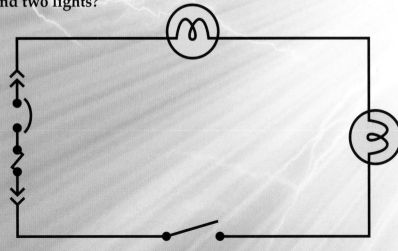

Other Series Circuits

Parts in electronics and appliances need different strengths of electricity to operate properly. Resistors in series circuits can bump up the electricity in part of the circuit, then reduce it later on. Resistors have small wires coiled around a ceramic core, which is a part in the center made of hardened clay. The number of coils and the way the resistor turns on and off can either increase or decrease the strength of the electrical current.

Series circuits are used in alarm systems. Contacts, or switches, are placed on windows or doors. When the alarm is set, electricity constantly flows through the circuit. When the window is opened, the contacts come apart, stopping the flow of electricity. This signals the alarm to ring.

What Is a Parallel Circuit?

A circuit with two or more pathways for current flow is a parallel circuit. Components each have a direct pathway to and from the power source.

Try It for Yourself!

Experiment

How do you build a parallel circuit?

Materials

- battery
- copper wires
- 3 or 4 bulbs

You might want to work in a group to build these circuits.

Procedure

1. Connect a short piece of insulated wire to each pole of the battery.
2. To these wires, connect a wire, bulb, and another wire to make a simple circuit.
3. Note the brightness of the bulb.
4. Connect another bulb and wires at the same connection, as shown in the illustration.

Continue with the procedure on the next page.

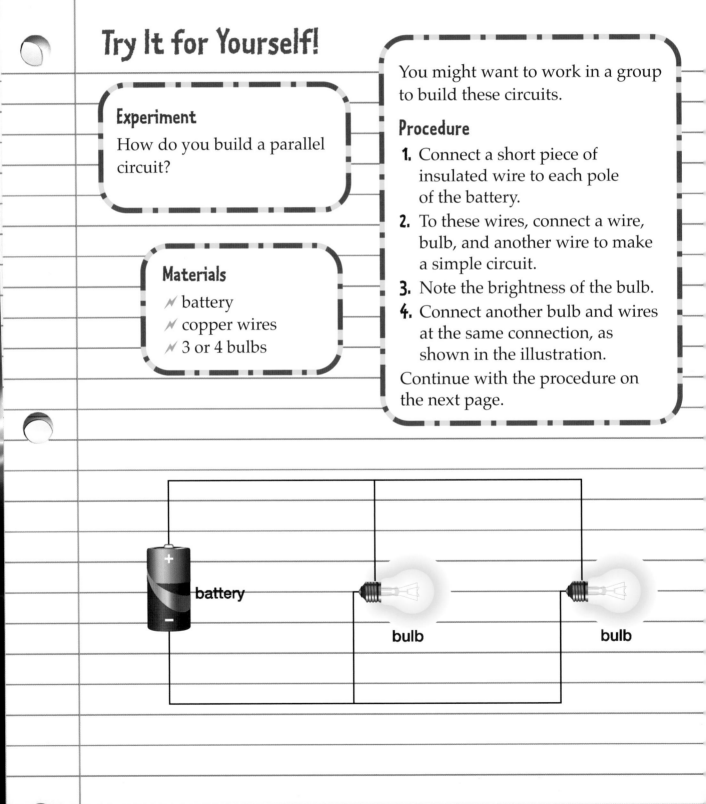

battery

bulb

bulb

Procedure

5. Wire in a third bulb in parallel.

6. Observe the brightness of the bulbs.

7. If you have a fourth bulb, you might even wire it in and see what happens.

battery

bulb   bulb   bulb

What Happened and Why

As you added new parallel loops to the circuit, the bulbs all stayed at the same brightness.

In parallel circuits, the electrical current can follow more than one path to return to the battery. In each parallel loop, the strength of the electrical current stays the same.

How Do We Use Parallel Circuits?

We use parallel circuits when we want elements in a circuit to receive the same amount of electricity. We use them when we want to make sure one element keeps working, even if the other burns out.

Heating Elements

Electric heaters and toasters contain parallel circuits. When you lower the lever on a toaster, the circuit is completed, or closed. Electricity flows equally to all of the heating elements. The heating element wires are part of one parallel circuit.

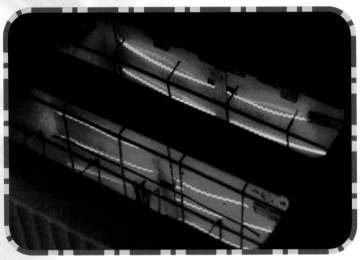

This two-slice toaster has four heating elements in a parallel circuit.

A schematic showing the four heating elements of a toaster in a parallel circuit looks like this.

Staying On

Parallel circuits allow other loads in the circuit to keep working even when one stops working.

The bulbs in a chandelier are wired as a parallel circuit. If one bulb burns out, the rest stay on because electricity keeps flowing to them.

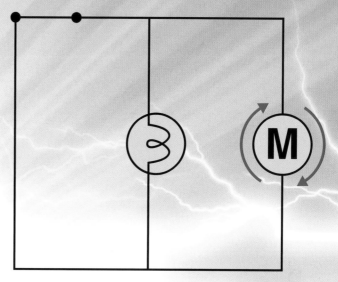

Many types of resistors, such as lights, speakers, or motors, can be wired in circuits. This schematic shows a bulb and a motor wired in parallel. If the light burns out, the motor will continue to run.

Complicated electrical devices, including most of our appliances, use both series and parallel circuits together.

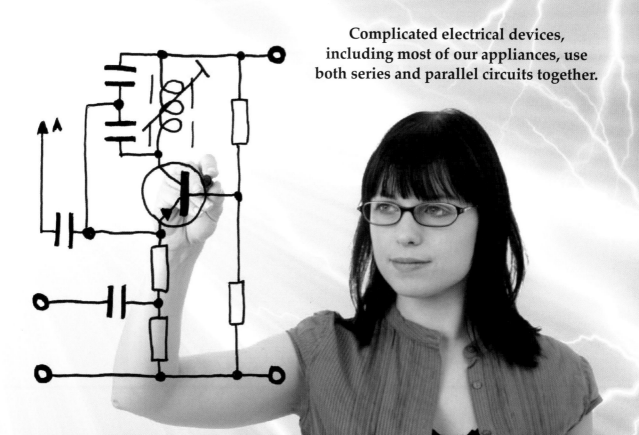

How Is the Electrical Grid One Large Circuit?

Electricity is transported along wires from power plants to businesses, factories, and our homes. This system of power lines is called the electrical grid.

The Electrical Grid

Large transmission lines carry electricity across long distances. Smaller transmission lines branch off to urban and rural areas. Smaller power lines, above or below ground, branch off to local neighborhoods. Wiring in buildings is connected to the entire grid.

When you turn on a light or an appliance in your home, you complete a circuit that stretches from your home all the way back to the power plant.

Electrical grids are huge, stretching across large regions. Grids interconnect with each other to cover entire continents.

This image shows the electrical grids that cover North America.

Grid Safety

For safety, the electrical grid has breaker switches at intervals along its entire distance. If a power line is hit by lightning, excess electrons trip the breaker. This opens the circuit so the power surge cannot follow the lines into homes and cause damage. If winds or an accident cause power line wires to touch and make a short circuit, the breakers will also trip.

A power line worker pushes a tripped breaker switch back into position.

Sometimes breakers shut down entire power grids. The eastern United States and Canada have had some memorable blackouts that left millions of people without electricity for long periods of time.

Flash fact

How Do Circuits in Your Home Work?

A house, condo, apartment, or trailer is wired with a number of circuits. Electricians follow strict rules when they install electrical circuits.

Household Circuits

Each circuit in your home begins at a breaker box that connects your household wiring to the electrical grid. From there, the circuit wires in the walls lead to every outlet, switch, and light.

Electricity can be dangerous, which is why governments create electrical codes. The codes are regulations about how circuits must be wired, and how many lights and outlets may be connected to each circuit. Electrical codes also tell electricians what types of wire and fixtures they should use. These regulations help keep people safe.

An electrician connects every circuit in a home to its own breaker in a breaker box.

This illustration shows one way this house could be wired. The circuits begin at the breaker box. Each circuit is connected to certain outlets and lights. This prevents circuits from becoming overloaded and tripping the breaker switch.

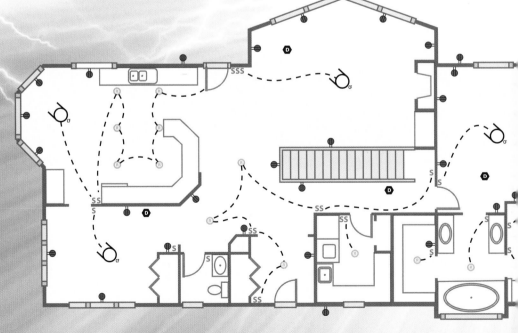

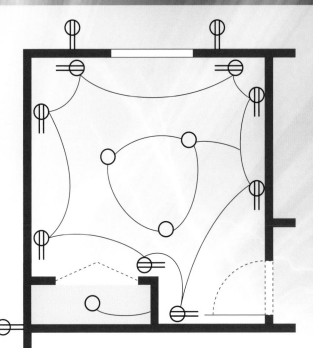

Your Home

When a building is being constructed, electricians are hired to install the wiring in buildings. They use schematics of electrical plans that follow electrical codes. The schematics show all the switches, lights, and outlets that will be in each circuit.

This schematic shows one household circuit. Can you tell how many outlets and light fixtures are wired into this circuit?

Try It for Yourself!

Investigation
What are the circuits in your home?

Material
- paper for recording
- pencil

Procedure
1. Do this investigation with the help of an adult.
2. Find the breaker box for your home's wiring and record the number of circuits you see.
3. Are they labeled, telling which part of your home each circuit serves?
4. Explore one of the circuits. Choose a circuit that does not lead to sensitive electronics. A bedroom circuit might be the best.
5. Find out how many lights and outlets are on that circuit. You can turn the breaker switch off and see which lights and outlets no longer have electricity.
6. Draw a schematic of that circuit.

How Can a Circuit Create Magnetism?

Electricity is closely related to magnetism. Electrical generators in power plants convert, or change, magnetic and mechanical energy into electrical energy. Electrical energy can then be changed to magnetic energy.

Generators

In a generator, an energy source turns a **rotor** that is surrounded by a **stator**. The rotor contains a coil of wire. Electricity goes through this coil and creates an **electromagnetic field** that surrounds the rotor. The stator contains coils of metal wires. As the rotor spins its magnetic field, the stator collects electrons from the magnetism and pumps them into power lines to your home.

Steam or moving water, which contain mechanical energy, push on the blades of a turbine. When the turbine spins, it moves the rotor in a generator.

Electrical Circuits Create Magnets

Every electrical current has a magnetic field around it. You can see the magnetic effect around an electrical circuit by moving a compass over a circuit wire.

If no electricity is running through the circuit, the compass will point to the north. When electricity flows through the wire, the compass will spin and point along the wire. It shows the direction of electron flow. The movement of the compass shows that the electricity flowing through the wire creates magnetism.

Electromagnets are created by winding wire from an electrical circuit around a core. This coil increases the magnetic effect. An electromagnet has positive and negative poles created by the direction of electron flow.

wire

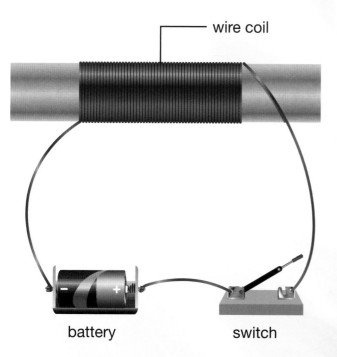

wire coil

battery

switch

You can build a simple electromagnet like the one in this diagram. Coil a length of uncoated wire around a pencil or narrow tube. Complete the circuit by connecting the wire to a battery and closing the switch. The coil now acts like a magnet and can pick up small metal items.

Flash fact

Electromagnets are the strongest magnets in the world. Some can lift cars or other heavy metal objects.

How Do Circuits Work in Everyday Objects?

Circuits do more than just carry electricity into machines, appliances, or electronics. You have seen how circuits create light and heat. They can also create movement and sound.

Electricity in a Circuit Can Create Movement

Electric motors can be huge or very tiny. They are used in factories, homes, and vehicles. All of them change electricity into mechanical energy—the energy of motion.

An electric motor is almost the reverse of a generator. In this diagram, electricity flows through a wire loop circuit between two magnets. The magnets cause the loop to begin spinning. The moving brushes act as switches. They make sure that electricity always flows into the left side of the loop. The magnetic field and the current push the left side of the loop down, and the right side of the loop up.

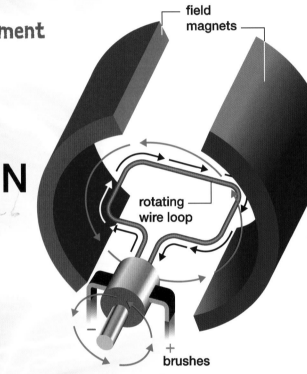

field magnets

N

rotating wire loop

brushes

The circuits in most electric motors use wire coils to increase their power. You can see the spin of these motors in items such as fans, electric mixers, washing machines, and car wheels.

This remote control car has small electric motors that change electrical energy into mechanical energy to move its wheels.

Electrical Circuits Can Create Sound

Loudspeakers range from huge arena sound systems, to TV and radio speakers, to tiny speakers in ear buds or hearing aids. They all use circuits and magnets to convert electrical signals into sound.

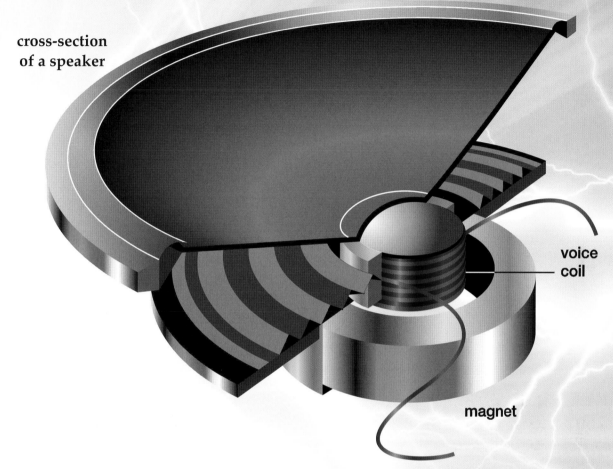

cross-section of a speaker

voice coil

magnet

The electrical signal flows through the speaker wire to an electromagnet called a voice coil. The voice coil sits in front of a magnet. The electrical current creates a magnetic field causing the coil to move back and forth quickly. The pressure of this movement creates sound waves. The sound waves are different shapes and sizes, depending on the volume and pitch of the music and voices you hear.

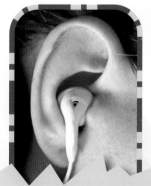

A cone attached to the voice coil makes the vibration bigger and passes these louder sound waves out into the air.

Flash fact

It is important to set MP3s at a low volume so the pressure does not damage your hearing.

How Do Silicon Chip Circuits Work?

Silicon is one of the most common substances on Earth. Silicon is a chemical element and is an excellent insulator, which is why it can be used as a base for extremely small circuits.

Making Silicon Chips

Silicon chips are so small that they are often called microchips. They can hold thousands of tiny electrical circuits. Silicon is mixed with other substances and used to print circuits on the chips.

Silicon is affected by very low electrical currents, which can open or close circuits, turning them on or off. By combining thousands and thousands of these on-off tasks, the chips can remember data and follow directions to perform many functions.

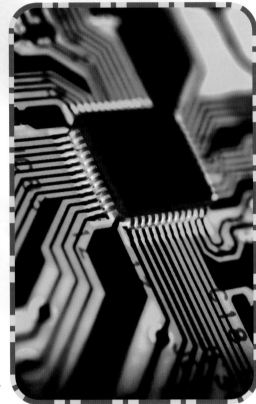

Silicon chips are placed in circuits on circuit boards in different ways to perform hundreds of tasks.

Uses of Microchips

Silicon microchips are used in many aspects of modern life. Chips allow for thousands of circuits in a very small space. They can also be manufactured cheaply.

Silicon chips are like little computers. They are used in microwaves, toaster ovens, and other appliances. They control the operation of larger appliances such as refrigerators, washing machines, and dryers, too.

Thanks to microchips, today's video games and MP3 players are often faster and more powerful than the largest computers of only a few years ago. Digital televisions and DVD players are possible only because of complex chip circuits. Silicon chips have made instant worldwide satellite communication possible.

Transportation also depends on chip circuits. In cars, they control how much fuel is burned. In airplanes, silicon chips measure information such as altitude, winds, and speed.

Microchips form the basis of complex circuits in all our desktop, laptop, and tablet computers, as well.

Scientists will continue to explore new methods of creating smaller and more powerful circuits in the future. Can you imagine what electrical circuits will be doing for us 50 years from now?

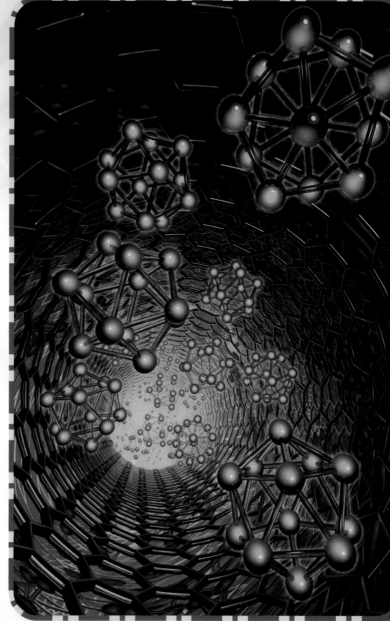

Nanotechnology is the science of creating devices on a microscopic scale. Can you imagine tiny robots powered by ever-smaller power sources swimming through you bloodstream to make you well? Scientists can!

Glossary

alternating current   Electrons moving in one direction and then reversing direction

battery   A container that stores a chemical mixture that can produce electricity

breaker   A switch that opens a circuit if there is an electrical surge or overload

cell   The simplest form of a battery

circuit   A route that returns to its starting point

conductor   A substance through which electrons easily flow

direct current   Electrons flowing in one direction

electrical grid   System of wires to transport electricity around the country; also called power grid

electromagnetic field   A physical field associated with electrical charge in motion, having both electric and magnetic components

electron   A negative particle circling an atom's nucleus

generator   A machine that produces electrical current

insulator   A substance that slows down or blocks the flow of electrons

load   A resistance in a circuit

parallel circuit   A circuit in which the current divides into two or more paths before recombining to complete the circuit

resistance   An element in a circuit that slows electrons

rotor   Rotating electromagnets in a generator

schematic   Diagram with symbols representing parts of a circuit

series circuit   A circuit with only one pathway for current flow

silicon chip   A small base containing tiny electrical circuits made of silicon

stator   Part of a generator that does not move. It collects and transports electrons.

switch   A device used to open or close a circuit

Learning More

FURTHER READING

Hydroelectric Power: Power from Moving Water (Energy Revolution). Marguerite Rodger. Crabtree Publishing Company, 2010.

Inventing the Electric Light (Breakthrough Inventions). Lisa Mullins. Crabtree Publishing Company, 2007.

Using Energy (Green Team). Sally Hewitt. Crabtree Publishing Company, 2008.

What Is Electricity? (Understanding Electricity). Ronald Monroe. Crabtree Publishing, 2012.

What Are Insulators and Conductors? (Understanding Electricity). Jessica Pegis. Crabtree Publishing, 2012.

What Is Electromagnetism? (Understanding Electricity). Lionel Sandner. Crabtree Publishing, 2012.

WEBSITES

The NASA SCIence Files™ Kids: Dr. D's Lab: "Electricity" Activities
http://scifiles.larc.nasa.gov/text/kids/D_Lab/acts_electric.html

SCIcentre Electrical Circuits
www.le.ac.uk/se/centres/sci/selfstudy/eam8.htm

JVC's Science Fair Projects
http://scienceprojectideasforkids.com/
Do a topic search for electricity. Many projects will come up about circuits and other aspects of electricity.

Index